the way the world comes in

pieces from

joesmith

pith...press

ISBN 978-0-9846059-1-0

FIRST PRINTING

pith...press
Gist Pith Ventilations
2309 E. Fernwood Ave.
Milwaukee, WI 53207

For Jenny, Dylan, Sophia, Maggie and Ally,
the loving family I don't deserve.

To Roy Arthur Swanson and Herbert Blau,
the finest mentors of mind I've ever known.

Contents

the way the world comes in

I'm singing, aren't I?

- Leonard Cohen

Holiday on the Farm

The soap opera organ announces
what we can hardly bear to hear.
Our metal-aproned matron
summons the skin ribbon
she left on the seat of a Galaxie 500,
circa 1969. Her tremolo
is a casual torture. We mistake
her voice for a choir of a thousand
veiled mothers and wobble dutifully
in to Easter dinner of wood duck
and greens. There are no roses
around our scarred 3D hearts
or arranged in the centerpiece
absorbing what words we can pick
from our teeth. We are weary, heavy
weary, of managed creation and sick
from songs that tempt us simply
to silence. We scrape cold beards
of frost with freshly buffed nails,
screeching at the April windows.
Our fathers were fools to store
their small-grained harvests
in such broad-slatted barns.
We watch the mess heap up
with the snow and the hyphens.
Nobody clears the faux-oak table
but the talkative furniture
does our dreaming for us
and a phatic nation learns to curse
in shrunken frontier tongues.

Leap

"It was intelligence and nothing else that had to be opposed."
- Søren Kierkegaard

The wind is against me
on my pedaled way to work.
A bus almost clips me
cutting in to its shelter at the curb.
A Benz would rather run the light and I
over than wait two seconds more.
The finger inside shows off its white
behind smoked, sloped glass. Every
car would rather rattle my irksome bones
across the avenue (like bar dice slammed
from their leatherette cup) than notice
I'm nearly naked without their metal
to hold me. I am only sure
winter will be worse and words
meant to comfort are drab impostures.

The wind again is against me
all the chilled way home. A horn
reminds me how much I need
a light to flash my presence. (More
would, of course, be better, but the bushes
here, if they burn at all, burn away to ashes.)
But I remember you said you had a "crush"
on me and I begin to wonder, in spite
of the wind and the traffic and the cynic
on my bike, how old is too old to feel
like a first-kissed kid blushing in public.
I can't help but think this
Spring might arrive a day or so early
or hear you when you say "It's ok. It's O. K."
I can even believe you mean each letter.

Versions to the World

I question the reach of your eyes in
front of the man who shaped no lean
sliver of who you are across from me
right now looking past me in your
wriggled chair and as for an answer you
bang your glass hard down at the table
almost slam it really splat on the
newspaper the high-pated president
asking us in that way that faces frozen
in mid-act wonder why intentions
wander off before reaching an eventful
end to their horizons on this washed
rock of a planet flung out to spin dry
some distance from an initial some
thing some cosmic shudder some single
odd nothing packed so hard in on itself
it just had to get away with us on it now
trying to pronounce the name of a wee
breakaway country where the man in
the picture lives beneath his small bone
wall of dug-in skin and up-creeping
eyebrows smearing down away to damp
but not gone and asking you me that is
not him to describe in some detail what
each of us are watching when we can't
quite look at one another and say
whether or not this will end for us in
three dimensions more or less in real
time yet tonight to make the movie we
both already heard about before an
arguable event hardens into matter and
carves its way into the crooks of our
eyes.

Cross Talk

Left hanging
will be a saying
in a mistaken destined nation
a millennium or two since my aching feet
and palms are ripped from this pedestrian piece of reused tree.

I thirst
for better revelations
than bumper stickers threatening
to free machines from their sins. Sorry
friends, no rapture comes to your four horseman town.

I am that I am,
a haggard rabbi with no thunderous
bush to hide my fiery parts, a *shmegege*
with a headache and a holey bag of rocks. I'm all
you've forgotten and never did like the music you made me.

Eloi Eloi
what the *lama sabachthani?*
Why the mystery? No mystery really
about a cuckold for a stand-in dad with a whole God
against him and mom nailed clearly by a conspiracy of stars

and moving,
always moving
from sung insult to sung
insult, from chicken yard to chicken yard.
Wherever we were, chickens & sand. I might as well be yellow

in Belgium
with dry-eyed nuns
staring down my bloodless toes
while a farmer fences their sisters. Know only
that I loved the feel of a breeze up my rough muslin skirt,

that the kingdom
is begotten within a sodden
you, that the sky is what can't hear you,
that my lot is but one willed coincidence to darken
what won't face me. Did it. Not bad. No visions. It is finished.

There

An abrupt abutment
of wide earth and broad air
is a line that draws him
without end to the boundary

of wide earth and broad air.
He plows a square on the plain
without end to the boundary,
the bent hedgepost by the sun.

He plows a square on the plain
he inherits and stares past
the bent hedgepost by the sun,
beyond a town, across the land.

He inherits and stares, past
an isolate tree and an elevator
beyond a town, across the land.
And on and along the horizon:

an isolate tree and an elevator
nothing save grain goes up.
And on and along the horizon,
the high hum from tall poles.

Nothing save grain goes up
from flat here. There is ever
the high hum from tall poles
from the coal mine to Chicago.

From flat here, there is ever
an abrupt abutment.
From the coal mine to Chicago
is a line that draws him.

a pantoum: a cyclically repetitive poetic form of Malaysian origin

Cacophony in A Minor, Op. 4, No. 13

Up in the pent apartment,
scarcely a story
away from an incidental
street, flush from another
neighborhood murder, at odds again
with the alleged moon. Hungry
but out of the essential soup, so
walking the way of all flesh
to the quick mart for coffee and reports in Arabic.
A targeted buyer of bottles and noodles
and improved antacids protected from little
in frayed tan shoes, attempting to edit
the insistent images, ever attendant
at the private screening,
portable, and wired
for cable. A concocted frenzy
of thin humor and wide desire
soaking in the predicted downpour, heading
nobody nor their errant horse off
at the heroic pass (though the western reruns
again at eleven). Alone
but not anonymous and never wholly
unaccompanied in the intentional city.
Preempting, weekly, the final arrangements
for what gathered ancestors could suppose by name.

In fits
and bursts,
in electric
magnetic outbursts,
from under the varnished door.
This is the way the world comes in.

Yet another era
among many.
Don't bother
to coin it.
This is not
a wanton garden
and we are hardly
our own origins,
nor am I
a woozy oracle
in an enigmatic state,
perched atop a tripod
above the vaporous stink
whipping up a riddle
in a piss-soaked bowl.
And no goat left that trail
reeking down the hallway.

Fluids in
and fluids
out, fumbling
for the keys
and dripping
on the landing.
A blooded
addendum
to what
but this
liquid
dubious
process,
an excess
again home
on rented
premises
to absorb
the news
unfiltered,
to inherit
a settled
territory
in an over-
crowded chair.

I call you on the cordless
and wonder out loud
if you could fix what's broken
and stuck to my bed.
You yawn and name it
me again, but still
you come and we eat
what's in. We're happy
to finish the other's
sentence and repeat our
stories at parties together.
Introductory dinners
require toothpicks
and napkins cribbed
with witty quips.

No. Didn't know him.
Just lived in the building.
Talked to the painter, though.
Splattered himself all over his own kitchen.
LAST CALL PEOPLE.
Like a Jackson Pollock.
Like a pot roast exploded.
Lost half-a-day scrapin' those brains off the walls.
Just painted over the littlest pieces.
NO MORE POOL.
Said he hopes they call him 'fore it dries next time.
Said psychics oughta quit reading cards.
The future's in the brains.
NO MORE MONEY IN THE JUKE BOX.
Wants to start his own business
DRINK UP PEOPLE.
paintin' crime scenes.
Gotta specialize these days.
YOU'RE OUTTA HERE.
Gotta plan ahead.

There is only water
Possum. No shadow
to speak of
and no rock
as far as anyone
remembers. Unreal,
maybe. But every city
implies its opposite
and there are no yeomen
here in frontier blue overalls
raising corn
or the dead.

Dark matter hums past us from the background.
The matter mostly missing, the dark guessed
at by the gravity of what is damn near there.

No matter,
no sense
of an ending
left on the seat
in mediis rebus
but senses
nonetheless
riding in the rolling advertisement
to the temporary agency
to impress the director
of human resources. Hanging
from the towel dispenser
may result in death or serious injury.

I tell
my self
I say
I am
not
and never
have been
too cruel.
The webcam
is a corollary
of medieval
conscience.
Believe you
tell me who
you are. I
make notes
of an absence
in the hefty
blue book
and refuse
to refuse
not to look.
Nothing is
more than
the case
it cannot
make for
you or itself.
No one goes
unpublished,
nothing is
yet unaired.

The water's churned in squat pools
beside the Great Lake, washed through
crushed cinders, piped beneath the real
estate, bottled and labeled in corrupt
or bent French. Spring rains season us
to taste. E. Coli is not the loan officer
who rejected your sister last winter.

No icons, no thank you,
no skin on our chicken,
no skeletal creed
upon which to drape
the meat of our days.
The waiter comes
when we can afford him
to tell us his name, to pour
more water and show us
his bones. He's a waiter
and he knows it. We're not sure
if we're dressed or wearing out
our welcome in magenta, red or fuchsia.

I've no faith in the tides
but cup my hands in the ocean
to see it seep through my cracks.
What washes to shore might
need a box or something like a vision.
Do not fear sailors (though
they're awfully wicked dealers), fear
the seas they grow sick from.
Suppose no future. Don't think
next year your odds for the Lotto
will be better. And don't stare.

Mister Charon, he left.
Got a view and two acres.
Polishes his Saab
every obvious Sunday.
Sells health insurance.
Panhandlers demand
more than quarters today.
The air is full of strangers
in rare communion. The ashes
on the mantle? Your mother's.
And a dozen others.
The undertaker got a subcontractor.
One clean-burning kiln for all.
We know better than to snicker
at the sadly-cramped commune
in the faux-golden urn.

Dark matter hums past us from the background.
The matter mostly missing, the dark guessed
at by the gravity of what is damn near there.

Drowning
without a buoy
to wave from
or wash broken up
on and no wet floe
to stand on or slide from
and no rock, no rock
to cover a delusion
or two. Drowning birds
on a nature show of
an African river.
A river is complicit
in all that I know
and I know it all
runs together, runs
through the room,
any room will do.
Drowning according
to the ceremonies
of shock that cannot hide
the ensured lack
of shadow or the fact
that nothing (save maybe
death en masse
and/or ex post facto)
shocks. Drowned sailors
take no shore leave.

We would rescue the tanked lobster
in our anniversary restaurant, feeling
his way along the clear walls, pointing
at us and every other seated hunger.
He's not picky, he's cooked. He's history
balled up in its own stiff juices,
saucy as a tomcat tossed in hell water.
We learn to maneuver from the Heimlich
poster and are glad to be extras
on this elaborate set, waving ferns
for the maker, our favorite auteur
filming Egypt from a boom truck,
parting the waters in a cracked bathtub.

A night out
for its walking.
Thank you for asking.
A healthy dollop
of what the fuck
chucked off the rooftop.
An aimless slick of disjecta
purged along the pavement.
A puddle of goo
behind the hatted statue.
No, I've never been
to a better Weltschmerz.
The singing was exciting
in any Asian language
and the costumes
almost blinding.
Goodnight. Say cher.
Très cher. Now.
With your eyes.

In fits
and bursts
in electric
magnetic outbursts
from under the varnished door.
This is the way the world comes in.

Charged
with nothing
but what
comes in so far
but what comes in
will not sit down
but finds a way
to somehow stay.
No deadlines yet
but feeling
something
like an editor
gnawing all fingers,
spilling the milk
before reaching
the cup, burning up
the plants and over
watering dinner,
craving something,
anything as solid
as iron (what
the universe yearns for)
to keep in a jar
or condemn with a fury
akin to conviction,
tuning in to every channel
predicting the millennium
will not be comic.
Locking the door,
a way the world comes in.

After Sonnets

Morning smells of everything we thought
to ask for. We turn over and breathe it
each away from the other in the smallest
tactful winds. The sun has beaten us up

again, but it's Sunday and we know nothing
demands us except the newspaper hefted
up to the stoop. I empty what night left
me while you remember your dreams leaning

against the doorway. We both know our days
are expected electric Christmas toys without
batteries and all the stores are closed.

But I flatten breakfast in the skillet as you pay
the electric bill and, after coffee, we bow
devoutly to a breathless love we never supposed.

Triptych (A Betrayal)

"Unable as yet to walk, or even to stand up... he nevertheless overcomes, in a flutter of jubilant activity, the obstructions... and, fixing his attitude in a slightly leaning-forward position, in order to hold it in his gaze, brings back an instantaneous aspect of the image." - *Jacques Lacan, "The Mirror Stage"*

\

My baby got up and marched back into the mirror from where he came. I would get at him with my every quivering tissue. I can't trust that he sucks the slow ooze from his mercury teether or explores the ear holes of his innumerable others. If there is but one lone baby, he is not me. If there are dense cities of babies enraptured by a magus in a winged skirt and floppy hat, I am far too many. In the meeting of mirrors on either side of the nerves I house, from both bends of planar sheen, familiar processions, not a baby among the disseminate hoards, approach. I turn away, pick my cuticles, and leave them to themselves.

|

Judgment is a waved dismissal. My double is disgusted by the 34x30 man I have taken from the rack. He unsnaps us, reminds me again that the personal pronoun is an insupportable ideal, and withdraws to the recess of his studied haunt. I'm beginning to think my baby is a fraud.

/

I have seen him at 70. He keeps his clothes and mothballs zipped up tightly, hangs them from a furnace pipe in their Naugahyde coffin of tasteful maroon, is not impressed with babies. He stutters across their screams, stammers over his 56 missions, his voice folding Dresden over, trailing off into the thin bang of a pocket stapler attaching sheets from the outside in. He saw the films later. He loathes the word homeless. He is prim in his brown fragrant suit, gathers litter from the sidewalks, sleeps in a temperate wood, feeds deer granola from his shaking palms, disappears for winter. Probably longer.

Nativity Scene

There are no camels in this combo crèche,
cooked in Singapore, assembled in Malaysia.
The pieces, each set in place, dominate the living
room, diverting our path to where we cleanse

and empty and I keep my store-bought teeth,
neither sneer nor smile in their snap-tight cup.
The lone cow's head is broken, decapitated
last season, lost in the vacuum or the latest

attempt to gather what mattered yesterday.
The wise men slipped off with the Barbies
on My Pretty Ponies. Mother Mary hides
her myrrh and secrets beneath a rigid chicken.

Cuckold Joe measures the cost of shame
by the size of his deductions. The Messiah,
in steep need of bowel relief, is inconsolable
in his ceramic straw cap. He's a baby, after all,

a baby gone angry with action-grip hands.
Any character that crawls across the gray terrain
is split at the jointed hip, fractured before seizing
the headless torso of the sole man doll, broken down

across the burro's back, loaded down as beasts will be.
Nobody is born here, really, nor gifts given
wholly, attached to hands as they are in the factory
plastic mold. Neither sheep nor shepherd will be
the same tomorrow. Reassembled as each must be.

The Back 40, Martin's House, 1969

When you asked me
where the boy went
I listen with the ears he left me.
He's not here
in the sounds
we each inherit
or the dinner down the hall
that sniffs around our room.
I have to catch him
past you, through
the pale square of paint,
through a nail hole that bore
a former tenant's portrait.

He's alone there,
still, beneath
the slant-roofed ceiling, peeling
slivers of old rose wallpaper
from anemic green plaster
older than both parents
added together, threading
the wall's dusty marrow
between his thumb and fingers
wondering how a house
could be ground down easier
than the best dirt in the world.

He points me out
through the window,
counts the miles
it takes
for electric
April cracks
to reach us,
says we can't cry
when yardsticks
shatter across his arms,
courtesy of Vernon's
Hardware and Mom
so mad, so far past
her prom dress picture.

He stops me
at the entrance
to his lilac hideout.
Leave him
to his aromas
and tin can collections.
He only wants
a dangerous fossil,
the hard press
of angry bone,
anything scarier
than a sandstone fern.
Next year, he rides
200 horses over forty acres.

He dares me to race him
down quarter-mile rows,
loses me running
through the wardrobes of corn,
their yellow hats rattling
over silky waist beards
sharp sleeves whipping welts
across his cheeks.
It would take days to find him
if he panicked. He can't,
like Dad, find faith
in the odor of heaven,
a promise of record harvests.

But he knows
grain claims air
from those who walk it
and nobody goes up
the only elevators he's seen.
His history's a river bottom
that floods every spring.
His summers confess
to nothing
but their sun.
He may come now
when you call him
and bring us his stare.

Cigarettes and Fish

Sealed in our amber conundrum
an arrested color to the world.

Our rooms are a mess of breath and tacks
a glossy photo with holes in four corners.

Dusk and sunrise are our times
deftly to operate the window shades.

We know snow comes from the west
filling in our angels the night we met.

Always there is a child in green anger
pajamas rattling at the crib posts.

We dry our memories like strips of hide
swollen along the slaughtered riverbank.

Girls will visit when we have finished
to save our words like sandstone ferns.

Boys will bring their fish-stabbing sticks
young cigarettes suckled by their cold sores.

We compose our still life on the carpet
an abstract of fish and forked restraint.

Our gestures parsed by the cut of lamp light;
we're simple subjects in the left hand corner

cradling ashtrays on the fourth floor landing.
There is our city. We were sick from it first.

Easter Week 2007

A corpse in a cowboy hat spews bile at the mike.
This time, he says he's an idiot.

A drove of men crowd around a bombed car in Karballah. All look
excited. Not one sad. 14 take pictures with their cell phones. The rest
appear to want a camera.

What does the Titanic have to do with Jesus?

You're a screen upon which all else is projected.
You wear your image of an image that looks almost like you.
Everybody watches. Nobody watches. You squint in such light.

Let the dead stay dead. Allow rumors of resurrection.

This method will back up all of your profile data for each profile in the
profile data location, as well as the registry.dat or profiles.ini file that
records the profile location. All profile data will be backed up at once,
together.

James Cameron. Hubris. Noun.

You won't speak to one of the several hundred of faces you glimpse
every day. See, they're pictures.

"The schizophrenic is not, as generally claimed, characterized by his
loss with of touch with reality, but by the obscene proximity to and
total instantaneous with things, this overexposure to the transparency
of the world."

Don Ho dies at 76. Hawaiian tourists will never be the same.

You see more of them if you don't leave the house.

The body of Christ. A thin thin wafer.
Stamped into a perfect circle.

1 in 4 Americans have a mental disease.
The other 3 are sick from thought.

Baker of Jesus crackers. There's a job.

Jackie Robinson. Somebody to believe in.

A woman in Idaho has had convulsive hiccups for 8 months.
"I believe in the power of Christ," she says.
"I've seen miracles MRAH-RRHHP happen."

C'mon, plaster Jesus, jump off that cross against the castle, snatch
the only man who gets to talk, shake him around in one hand, toss
him out to the crowd. Scare us.

"In spite of himself the schizophrenic is open to everything...."

The total player salaries who wore number 42 was 147.3 million.

Tell us a parable.

A state trooper in Kentucky was driving in a rainstorm
when he hit a horse and rider on an unlighted rural highway.

"He is the obscene victim of the world's obscenity."

The rider was charged with DUI of a non-motorized vehicle.

Tell us you meant something else.

The horse was euthanized at the scene.

C'mon, you can do it. You're 9 feet tall.

(Quotations from Jean Baudrillard, The Ecstasy of Communication)

Beauty is too skinny

We abandon what merely annoys us, take
our faba and melon alone and early
in such as light as the curtains allow, purchase
the weather from checkered gentlemen,
sketch lilies in the margins of unread flight novels
and barely speak of how our days went.

C'est la.
Take the print
from that wall.
It is far
too patent.
Hang it
over the antique
chifforobe, near
the finches.
It will echo
the colors
in their cage.
Our motives
are apparent
as our manner
of shoes
is learned.

There is no music here
save that which winds
your necklace tight.
You twist a fingered imitation
of Möbius, strip gently
an oyster from its open shell,
tap your foot slightly
like your mother
and bemoan her
taste in stony gardens.
I tell another story, quit
smoking and wear myself
like a pedaled machine.

Say la. Oooh
this certainly is
the new man denied
before us, more ad
vantageous for the film
we're in and simply
wet with worthy.
Pour les femmes
nous croyons, our visions
drawn by hands shifting
hairy in the softened
glare. A man is easier
to mold into a door
than to look at with this
much wonder. *Viens-tu.*
Tiens toi là.
Show us
the lighting
behind the fine
fine angles, the
lines pinched inside
the leanest shadows of you.

So blasé, the fat absentee
wiring a preference to the auction.
He is an artful office of rich
thick wool wound about the ankles
of makeshift lovers. They may
know a riddle and he wants
its name. We erase our faces'
creases with red styptic pens,
skin the peelings from our apples
and caw, when cornered, like mottled bitterns.

Oooh... La. La.
She is cleaner
than a mother
goddess, and wanton
as a peasant, drunk
at the harvest
festival, yet
finely so textured
and very well
mounted. More
than just a whistled
vision and brighter
than a primal
mask. And shaped, oh,
no demanding abstraction
or intrusion of colored
idea. No nervous
German this one; he had
a keen and steady hand
and placed on her
the correct amount
of breasts. *Voila*
mes frères, hypocrites
lecteurs. Ooh ooh and oh so la.

Tonight we buy.
We buy an ounce of odor.
We buy much and long
coats of favorite animal.
We want, again,
to endow our possible
limps with the lithe redemption
of hide. We cover
ourselves in the nimbly felled,
in blacks and browns, in chosen
homes of nearly wood. If we
could see beauty as clearly as
the hairs we trim weekly,
we might stop bending
into magazines which ask
for nothing but our envy,
our awe, our firm pursuit.
We might lose then
these breezy lobbies
that make us wait, that play
us. always, taut as catgut
over mauve violins.

What a palaver
these instruments
strewn about the band shell.
The minstrels of blue
have shut their lockers
at the station and left
whole gangs of echoes
to wander the tunnels, playing
fugues for crippled quarters,
cradling papered bottles
to soothe the din of afternoon.
A sad *Selah.* Our stories
are neither about ourselves
nor beyond our nailed ceilings.
There are colors
rawed in the hallway
and guitars in the kitchen
twanging inane rebellions,
the hits from days we surely
romanced or imagined.
We burn like flagged targets
in a blown sandy country
and scan the courtyards
for sculpted children
memorizing their phases of moon.
Ours may have lost their desire
to play like waves and sparks.

We dress darkly
and nothing of
the night surprises.
We mute its sirens by hanging
yards of grey-flecked drapes.
We count the roses
in a heavy delivered vase
and control the show's volume
from the couch at ten paces.
We read of an emaciated carpenter
with awl holes in his palms;
he's thin and set between panes
of glass, suspended in urine
and more than once named lovely.
Don't bother to shock us.
We're inured of shock, though
we know of bearded censors
and their casual cigars.
We are more than often
no more than amused.
What is immediate
we name knowledge.
We are politic, and can
spell, with some assistance,
abandon and aesthetic.

Light,
more light.
We must
have light.
This is the art
of the lesion
on the classical
mask. Our
hope
is a tragic
lack
in blankets,
to cover
the darkness,
to illumine
our room at night.
We misquote
the whole
known universe
and mistake
the sublime
for fruit
or time.
We have not
begun to define
our limbs' uses.

Prediction

On the Chinese calendar

In the year of the Pig

I am a Rat

Alert.

Zeno Whole

I have to save spaces.
No, I'm no wigged surveyor
with a three-legged stare
bent over destiny, unsettled
by innominate expanses, done
in by an absence of fences,
sectioning up the plenty.
We know how that was
manifest. I am not
enamoured of wrought
geometries and plaid
is a sad parody of place.
I save only spaces:

triangulate spans between
the bridge trusses where
swallows play no-touch tag,
the cracks under windows
where the winds whistle in,
those gaps around the sink
where prehistoric beetles
pass like Hermes from world
to world, the lulls in a song
where notes go to compose
themselves, the fissures
in a hammerhead stamped
out of tempered metals.

I make a man inhabit
the middle of this room
and wait to arrange nothing
but occasions to empty.
When he's finished fashioning
a sound container, we carry
slim air wherever needed:
to earthquakes and murders,
to bend the paths of bullets
and reverse the sad collapse
of width. Yes, I suppose
I have to catch him first.
A space is for saving.

Waukesha Tattoo

Here in the town of the common
and the good, only the flashes
reach us. There's no thunder
rumble, no sound to savor,
no low music to score
the out-of-favor soul. No, first
it's the din, carried air away east, then
the bright, the flight of sand as light,
breaking in waves on main street curbs
where memories are two blocks long.

Homines urbis mundi,
park in the lines diagonally.
Turn right or left one-way
at the pagoda that would be green.

A yo-yo in the hand of the boy on the bike
who ups and downs for most the day,
metal in his head and a knack, at ten,
for squaring every stimulus. Not much to do
for the dudes at Dave's Music. They swap names
of shared lays, grow their hair pretty long
and each one knows where the other one lives.

The name came
from their language.
Not the painted faces.
Not the whooping fans of earth.
Never the poxed and slaughtered remembered.

A caudal of the flocked strain hymns
through their steepled hole of sky:
grace notes for toothless grinding,
lung gurgles for the oligarchy.
We need this town like you need that tattoo,
a black widow you designed yourself
for Bill the Renaissance Needle to etch.
A helluvan artist, says the 'Nam vet
with the vulture on his knee.

We barter our hearts like borrowed garments
and run to each other as slow-mo lovers
in a misfed reshoot of a colorized film.

This all must please
the keepers of the grids
that plot our soddled odds
and finagled every street.
We watch the parabolas
full up across the sky,
the tired arc as rising star,
as arbitrary schism between ground
and map to zero. We're as gods,
we are. Less their entertainments.

Le dessin t'y manifeste.
C'est un mauvais geste.
Oh Lord, it do so work
in sleep and less awake ways.

Barophobia

Day climbs the pine
through the window you wanted me
to wash last spring from the neighbor's borrowed ladder.

Morning is quiet like this
before rushing us through routines
of water and coffee and out to what day invariably makes of us.

You know I need
this morning silence, that I need
silence more silent than silence can contain, that I won't admit

this as such requires
speech, that pain is what I say
we imagine, that I imagine it could stay hidden under a pillow,

that any given case
is all the case that the world can be,
that you can't let me stay too long in the silence where alone

is as alone as alone
must be, as you reach for my warmest
spot, doing your best to slide the wake from what can't hear

the crackle of cones
across snow, to rattle he who fears
neither heights nor pines, but quakes at the sight of landing.

Sonnet

Alert as the light that changes color
with the weather atop the building
most mistake as electric, we are mingling
our blood and juices without the dolor

that ought to accompany a great big age
of disease. We are lovely here and welcome
the changes we bring to every brown room.
In the phone booth, we are tearing our pages

from the musclebound book, feeding each
to the other our spare and crinkled names.
Ecstasy is this, and we, we are sudden
and hairy on the fair political body.

We are slick in the acidic rain, slippery
as a morning mood. We bite and wrestle
like wiry otters, loving mud and burning
wet without a stick of weathered wood.

View

Sequestered in a slim room,
television pawned, green
salad eaten, fork and plate
air drying, rent a week
overdue, she affords herself
the moments (though hours
tonight are inflationary,
swollen to moonish proportions)
for listening to the music refuse
to arrange itself in her presence.

The gift (from a birthday
lover, a grounded sailor fresh
out of directions) sits, collecting
dust on the dresser, its small
body a cavern demanding spaces,
hungry to stuff itself with quiet
urges, collecting her slightest
gestures, moving her to the window
to find the moon through the thick
frost, low over the twitching light.

Tonight is a wide reminder of longer
desire, sight a cramped and angry
animal. Tomorrow she pawns a camera.

Summertime

She is assuredly alone
in the dumbest of the seasons.

The hot pavement and masonry
frame her. The sun, a fiery voyeur,

its rays violations, leers
from another incomplete height.

The shadows she exits are severe,
sharp and linear as the darkest argument.

She looks east, toward light, not for direction
but to defy all that is flat and massive.

The chiseled lines of the architecture
are peeved at her curvature. She takes

the stairs away. Only one window's breeze
approaches her easy endurance, brushing

the curtains, wishing she would notice.
Confined in white, white whiter than suns

or washed monuments, she is motion itself
in a mannish hat. She leads with her dignified

thigh, out of urban geometry. She is no man
or artist's daughter, mistress of neither son nor slab.

(After Edward Hopper's "Summertime" for which his wife, Jo, was the model.)

Arse Poetica

I'm host to a party in a small space with a wide window and a high door shaken from its hinges some years ago. If pressed, I'll admit I invited several guests and inherited more than a few. but there are too damn many men in this too tiny space to serve them all at once.

The man in blue flannel pajamas is convinced of a conspiracy against all who aren't in on the whole complex mess most mortals can't grasp yet contribute to by breathing. When I can make myself concentrate, I can't follow the course of his rambling particulars, but I do admire his pajamas, both their blue and the feel of their flannel.

The guy without a god, but an impulse -- It moves, he says, in the blood -- to have faith -- and unmanaged air. -- in it all -- Why not try? -- if only in the mind -- A fire to tend. -- whispers "verily verily" before every proposition and "Selah" after, upchucks in the ficus, apologizes to the wall, and shaves his fedora with a disposable razor.

The boy who takes in strays and bottle feeds them back to health is inconsolable over losing a raccoon. The junkie offers him apple juice and a fresh set of works. The cynic with the permanent smirk smacks him on the back, shoves a Cohiba in his mouth, and laughs "Fuck inner children. What dies inside makes me stronger."

The sentimentalist stands in a corner, sniffling over Dumbo's mother. He's unpopular with the heavy drinkers. The medievalist scholar on Grail quests tries to talk to him, but can only ask "What ails you?" The ex-farmer with the pain-induced stare scratches his absence of arm and warns all of the dangers of an Archimedes screw.

The journalist says America is the best car wreck ever. He reports its screams before someone else does. The worried dad knocks scotch from his hand and threatens him with the wrath of Christmas past. The armchair physicist announces the universe as void without us to watch and the cryptologist rearranges the refrigerator magnets.

The gambler and the actuary argue over the odds of a widespread Rapture panic. The Buddhist and the hedonist agree on ends but part ways over the means to burn desire up or down. The acid-addled punk frees the clipped-wing finch, pats its head a little and promptly kicks it at the biographer before beating him senseless.

The populist sneers at the elitist but makes change for his hundred dollar bill. The aphorist and the logician misquote Wittgenstein in unison. The lovesick seller of foreign flowers trades baseball cards with the atheist and everyone mocks the feminist father of three beautiful daughters.

I don't want to humor their collective delusion. They're not the faulty antenna of the whole human race and don't I know it, but I serve them because a host is a host to a guest and a guest is a parasite and a parasite is, well, what the hell else?

Continuum

She said she was time,
the rich and widowed heiress,
and I, the toothless fornicator,
think a lot of space.
Oh, the usual two-step
turtle-to-bunny conundrum
and Kansan butterflies predicting
the New York weather.
I said I believed
time was hourglass
but you are melon and lemon.

Decant the wine
say *trés trés cher*.
The old is poured
comme ça.
Rah Rah
in to shiny bottles.
Do not worry.
A barren nation
has plenty of ice.

So she said that
and I say this
and time was
and time will mostly just be
and space is vast
where the curs rut
ruthless in the Detroit car
it's raining streets and the lights
are alit across boulevard filth.
We are no union of moon and mesa.
But we're assuredly skilled at making do.

In Tongues

Whatever they were, maybe "Winter
was the worst invention," maybe "Where
is the corner of Locust and Oak," maybe
En arche en ho logos, who knows...
Words are what got us here and words will keep us
when we've finished narrating the neighborhood air.

Wafting always around us, watching us watch
them warp the sunlight, wanting us, wanting
us to catch them, mixing our air and metaphors,
telling us when to talk and when not, making us
burrow for them in the hollows of our ears,
deep into the sweet and noisy meats of us.

We're parables dropped in the dirt, manic
Kabbalists abase with faith, drunk in the breath
of Shekinah, awash in the sense of one another
and we mean what we wash, from under our secret
folds, supping seas of aboriginal relatives, taking
the Nazarene, that wily near savior, seriously: Take, eat,

this is luscious and flesh and words which become us,
passing through as surely as gravity demands
us through the floorboards, as easily as neutrinos
waft through us by the minute, by the millions, the echoed
afterbirth of a raucous universe, the guests left over from
a haunted party, the last wee bastions of beauty and oblivion

Science Lessons (for Dylan)

When you asked me where the sun went
at night, I wanted to tell you the universe
tucks its rounded zillions of roving children
to bed in more ways than we could ever count
on all the fingers of a hard peopled earth.
I wanted to say your wonder is better
than a thousand answers, to say questions
hollow hideouts where you're safe to imagine.
But dads are doomed to explanation.
So we searched for every lost ball in the house,
collecting them with the dustballs and coins under
the chairs and the sofa, from behind the most amazing
refrigerator in the cosmos. We made a model
of the scattered planets across the living room carpet.
I held the wiffleball sun and tried to make the green
rubber earth spin slowly as it circled its necessary friend.
We learned that Dad is a lousy contortionist.

When you asked me where light comes from
without the flick of forbidden switches, I wished
I would have said that you invented it
your own sweet self, that you send it out
to every shadowed thistle on the vacant lot
around the corner. But instead I said
it was made in the compacted playgrounds
of big burning stars, that it's faster than airplanes
or race cars or the wits of poets who believe
their own pointed voices, that sometimes it flies
like a weiner roast spark and sometimes it waves
like the foaming blue ocean or like Daddy
when he misses the frisbee you throw him.
I should have told you how a photon finds
its one loving other through a pinhole in a wall
the size of Australia. A lab full of all the fathers
in the world couldn't explain why that's my favorite.

When you asked me how kittens are born,
I told you Mom and Dad animals are friendlier
in Spring. But I remembered the horrible wails
of feline heat, that a tomcat has a nasty barbed penis,
is chased away after quick and vicious union,
but comes back to attack its own blind, hidden babies.
I decided that one could wait until later,
at least until Dad understood it a bit better.
So you heard a wise story with something like a moral,
how the life of a cat shut up in a box depends
on the people outside. Inside, it's a wonder, incredibly
both dead and alive. But if someone pries open
the privacy of its shelter, it has to be one, or
worse, the other. The fury of curiosity
can be deadly for a kitty. I want to promise
that Dad won't let anyone pry open your boxes.

Utility

When I'm done, love,
when the impalpable me has made
his sullen exit, scrape clean
the meat from my bones. String it
in taut thin ribbons with piano wire
between the limbs of a lone oak
a last owl has been rumored to visit.
Wait for the end of morning rain.
Listen to the doves summon
their hunched brethren, the shunned
ones, the odoriferous ones, the old
utilitarians who speak to no one
but share their senses of humor
and occasion with cackling jackals.
They are wise to gorge on what
rots in vain remembrance.
Then turn and hum
a tune of your own invention.
Ignore that slight song at your back
and follow your salted path home.
Rend there my considerable fat.
Sow it along the mudslick riverbank
for the wading birds to pick at.
It may increase their wanting
knees. Strew easy my compliant
bones around an open field
in the shapes of some ruined alphabet.
Write witty aphorisms. Form
curses toward the sky. Reserve
a single fibula for sharpening
the knife with which you mince
our girls' green meals.
Make use of me. Please.

de trop

Half full of someone like his mother
or her lover in dad's traveling robe.
Turned in an instant to the strained grace
of pointed cameras, a kleptomaniac
of attention, eyes pinched in lit aluminum,
hoarding his latest memory loss
in a cipher nation of nervy oblivion,
entertaining what remains of the children.

Bozo is staring at his shoes again,
doing his damnedest to shape his mouth
around gratuitous clearly, scratching
lotto tickets at the high white counter,
slurping up the bottom from a Monster
Superstar cup, wondering where
he goes to cash in his principals
and who made off with his only Sunday suit.

His conception was an overnight
talk show. Celebrities appeared
to watch from the work shirts behind
the louvered doors. He knows he's responsible
for the poor reception, but the moon
is no klieg light and he's usually
out of film. He wants to edit his inheritance,
stuff his finger up the aperture, sleep through
to morning. No. Make that afternoon.

Plowing

At night, you know
the directions if you look

at the sky. See where the sun was,
then you'll know where you're going.

On the absolute plain
on the leveled little hill,

the soil real, the rise artificial,
trucked in from township ditches.

Family picked the cans out,
threw their seed around

and began to stare.

In the dark
in a trance

in a stance like
and so beside Daddy,

you think
you're called

by something further, something
past the grain-gorged sentinels.

Stone white phalloi poking the sky.

At twelve, proud and rattling
in the tractor. Find a tree

if you can, son. If not, strike a line
toward the tallest bone of corn,

toes tangling air like Jesus
scared godless on the water.

Pulled
in every

where
you look.

So young, so slashing
gashes in the loam,

a crescent man
with dad and iron

on his side, turning everything
but your mother under.

In the cold before April, he'll go like a gaze.

Handicap

A man and his backbone

are dangerously exposed.

Perhaps this explains

a shortage.

Stream 4.3

There are icons to shatter here.

Does anyone remember when meaning was meaningful?

Don't condemn the meta. It's all we have left. And it might hear you.

People are not stupid.

"We no longer have anything to hide in this integral reality that envelops us."

They are oblivious.

I am of two or more minds.

You can't feel up unless you get down.

"To what in the virtual universe can one feel an obligation?"

Suicide is a state of mind.

As a social phenomenon, the pursuit of small celebrity is not terribly phenomenal.

You have to keep it alive.

All organisms must purge themselves of the negative, the threats to survival, the obstacles to their reproduction.

Is America freedom's end game?

The threats from within.

I have a tremendous capacity for joy.

But I am saving it for the apocalypse.

Life is a fine place to go grocery shopping.

I'd be more troubled by my duplicity if I weren't so ambivalent.

In the trial of the mind, every voice receives a hearing.

The most broadly accepted human falsehood, around which whole cultures, religions & belief systems are constructed? That we matter.

And the jury is hung.

I think in B flat minor.

Nothing.

"We are in a state of total agnosticism with regard to the existence of reality, with regard to ends and ultimate meaning."

To hold on to.

I half intend almost half the words heard in my head.

Grip tightly.

Admiration is an empty activity.

Fuck it. None of this makes any bloody sense. - Ludwig Wittgenstein

I do not admire an abundance of people who are alive.

Waxing philosophical.

It could take hours to come.

Depressives last longer.

About the Author

joesmith is of type: person
joesmith is your login ID
joesmith is not OK
joesmith is ex nihilo
joesmith is gnu bash
joesmith is not Joe Smith
joesmith is 1960
joesmith is hickie
joesmith is nada
joesmith is child
joesmith is normal rights
joesmith is an active warrior in the warriorforum
joesmith is add post to del
joesmith is from Christian County
joesmith is no thing
joesmith is a user of x
joesmith is not master
joesmith is emptying his warehouse of craft supplies
joesmith is no Mormon
joesmith is black time
joesmith is unsteady flux
joesmith is city
joesmith is in #discussion on efnet
joesmith is confined
joesmith is Nihil
joesmith is Dada
joesmith is 1968
joesmith is basement
joesmith is all in
joesmith is haunted mansion
joesmith is domesticated
joesmith is off line
joesmith is unimproved
joesmith is unavailable
joesmith is insta
joesmith is nothing new
joesmith is blip
joesmith is not Joseph Smith
joesmith is unfounded
joesmith is fall

With gratitude and acknowledgement for previous publication of these pieces in the following fine literary journals:

Crux - *Cigarettes & Fish, Leap, Zeno Whole*
The Iowa Review - *Versions to the World*
Pavlov Neruda - *View, Zeno Whole*

82

pith...press

Gist Pith Ventilations
Milwaukee / New York